Smokestacks
and Spinning Jennys

Sean Price

Raintree

Chicago, Illinois

© 2007 Raintree
an imprint of Capstone Global Library LLC
Chicago, Illinois

Customer Service 888-363-4266

Visit our website at www.heinemannraintree.com

Designed by Michelle Lisseter, Kim Miracle, and Bigtop
Printed by CTPS

15 14
10 9 8 7 6 5

**Library of Congress
Cataloging-in-Publication Data**

Price, Sean.
  Smokestacks and spinning jennys : industrial revolution / Sean Price.
      p. cm. -- (American history through primary sources)
  Includes bibliographical references and index.
  ISBN 1-4109-2413-0 (hc) -- ISBN 1-4109-2424-6 (pb)
  1. Industrial revolution--United States--Juvenile literature. I. Title.
II. Series.
  HC105.P95 2007
  330.973'05--dc22
                                          2006006581

13-digit ISBNs
978-1-4109-2413-1 (hardcover)
978-1-4109-2424-7 (paperback)

Acknowledgments
The author and publisher are grateful to the following for permission to reproduce copyright material: Bettmann/Corbis **pp. 11**, **13**, **22**, **24–25**, **26**, **27**, **28**; Corbis **pp. 15**, **19**, **20**, **21**, **23**, **29**; Getty Images **p. 9**; The Granger collection New York **p. 10**; Mary Evans Picture Library **p. 7**; Museum of the City of New York/Corbis **pp. 4–5**; Sean Sexton Collection/Corbis **p. 16**.

Cover photograph of metal workers in a factory reproduced with permission of Sean Sexton Collection/Corbis.

Photo research by Tracy Cummins.

The publishers would like to thank Nancy Harris and Joy Rogers for their assistance in the preparation of this book.

Every effort has been made to contact copyright holders of any material reproduced in this book. Any omissions will be rectified in subsequent printings if notice is given to the publishers.

Disclaimer
All the Internet addresses (URLs) given in this book were valid at the time of going to press. However, due to the dynamic nature of the Internet, some addresses may have changed, or sites may have changed or ceased to exist since publication. While the author and publishers regret any inconvenience this may cause readers, no responsibility for any such changes can be accepted by either the author or the publishers.

It is recommended that adults supervise children on the Internet.

Contents

Some words are printed in bold,**like this**. You can find out what they mean on page 30. You can also look in the box at the bottom of the page where they first appear.

What Was the Industrial Revolution?

The clue is in its name. The word **industrial** has to do with making things. A **revolution** is a time of great change. So, the Industrial Revolution was a time of great change in making things.

This exciting time began around 1760. Before 1760 many families worked on farms. They grew their own food. Few people back then used machines.

Before 1760 most families ▶ made their own clothes, tools, and houses.

factory — building where products are made
industrial — anything that has to do with making products (things that are made and sold)
revolution — time of great change

The Industrial Revolution changed all that. There were new machines. These machines made things quickly. Many things were made inside large buildings called **factories**. People could buy what they needed instead of making it.

Machines such as trains made going from place to place easier. People left their farms and small towns. They moved to cities instead. The Industrial Revolution changed daily life.

New Inventions

Spinning wheels are used to make thread. They make thread from cotton or wool.

James Hargreaves was a weaver in England. A weaver is a person who makes cloth. Hargreaves had a daughter named Jenny. It is said that one day Jenny knocked over the family's spinning wheel. The year was 1764.

Spinning wheels can only make one thread at a time. Jenny's accident gave Hargreaves an idea. He created a machine that could make many threads at once. He called it the **spinning jenny**.

By 1778 there were 20,000 spinning jennys in England. This machine made it easier and faster to make cloth. Cloth making started the Industrial Revolution.

spinning jenny   machine that spins several threads at once
spinning wheel   wheel used to make thread
textile mill   building with machines that make cloth

▼ *The spinning jenny could make several threads quickly.*

Francis Cabot Lowell was an American businessman. Lowell visited English **textile mills** Textile mills are buildings with machines that make cloth. Lowell studied how the machines were built.

Then Lowell made his own cloth-making machines. Lowell built his own textile mills in Massachusetts. He helped bring the Industrial Revolution to America.

Interchangeable parts

In the past, items such as chairs were made one at a time. A **carpenter** made them. A carpenter is someone who makes things with wood. This work was slow. It cost a lot of money. Also, two chairs may look the same, but they were not. The legs or arms might be different sizes.

Eli Whitney saw a faster way to make things. Around 1800 he **invented** (created) **interchangeable parts**. That means all pieces used to make something are exactly the same size. They are also the same shape. For example, the leg on one chair could be changed out for the leg of another. This system was called the **American System**.

The American System changed the way things were built. Several people did the work instead of just one. Each worker handled a single step, such as adding the seat to a chair. The American System was faster and easier. It was a cheaper way to make things.

American System	way of using interchangeable parts to produce goods
carpenter	someone who makes things with wood
interchangeable parts	parts that are the exact same size and shape
invent	create something that has never been made before

◄ Eli Whitney's system helped change how products are made.

9

Steam engine

On August 17, 1807, people first saw a boat called the *Clermont*. The *Clermont* had a **steam engine**. The steam engine heated up water. This made steam. The power of the steam could push and turn things. It turned a giant wheel. The wheel moved the *Clermont* forward.

▲ *Smoke from the* Clermont's *engine left a trail of dark clouds.*

steam engine   machine that heats up water to make steam

Robert Fulton put the steam engine on the *Clermont*. It was soon steaming up and down the Hudson River in New York. People were amazed. They had never seen a boat move so quickly going up a river. "The whole country talked of nothing but the [*Clermont*]," one person said.

Several people **invented** the steam engine used on the *Clermont*. One of those people was James Watt. Watt's steam engine powered boats and trains. It also powered **spinning jennys** (machines that spin thread) and other machines.

Robert Fulton was one ▶ of the first people to put a steam engine on a boat.

Trains and railroads

On December 25, 1830, a group of people got a special surprise. They rode on *The Best Friend of Charleston*. This was one of the first U.S. trains. It was reported that everyone enjoyed the ride:

"[The passengers] flew . . . at the speed of 15 to 25 miles [24 to 40 kilometers] per hour," the newspaper said. Today, that speed would feel slow. But back then, few people had traveled so fast.

First U.S. train

The first train in the United States was built in 1825. It was built in Hoboken, New Jersey. It ran on a track laid out in a big circle. Its owner just wanted to see if it would work.

railroad   business that uses trains to move people and things

Soon, the **railroad** business began. Railroads carried people. They also carried things. Trips that once took weeks could be done in hours or days. People could travel quickly. They could spread news more quickly than ever before.

Before trains, people▼ walked or rode horses.

Fuel of the Revolution

Most of these new machines needed **fuel**. Fuel is something that is burned to provide power. It also provides heat. The main fuel of the Industrial Revolution was **coal** Coal is a type of black or brown rock. It burns well.

Coal was perfect for running **steam engines** Steam engines are machines that heat up water to make steam. The power of the steam can push and turn things. Burning coal heated the engine's water to create the steam.

Oil

*Over time, **oil** began to replace coal as fuel. Oil is a dark liquid that burns well. Automobiles need oil to work properly. When cars became popular in the early 1900s, so did oil. But burning oil makes the air dirty as well.*

coal   black or brown rock that burns well
fuel   something that is burned to make power or heat
oil   dark liquid that burns well

Textile mills used coal to power machines. **Factories** used coal, too. People burned coal for heat. But burning coal made the air dirty. It caused thick, black smoke.

▼ *This man is working near a coal mine.*

15

Iron and Steel

People made many **products** during the Industrial Revolution. Products are things that are made and sold. People also made machines. They used **iron** to make the machines strong. Iron is a metal.

▼ *These men work in an iron factory.*

Abraham Darby found a cheap way to melt iron. Then the iron could be shaped easily. It could be made into useful products. Once it cooled, iron was tough. It lasted a long time. Iron replaced wood in bridges and buildings.

Iron was also used to make parts for machines. Soon, people combined iron with other metals to make **steel**. Steel is an even stronger metal.

Farmers put steel blades on their **plows**. Farmers used the plows to plant seeds. The new plows were tough. They made planting easier. Farmers could plant more seeds.

iron	tough metal that is easily shaped when hot
plow	tool used to cut the ground for planting crops
product	thing that is made and sold
steel	strong metal created by combining iron with other metals

Working for a Living

During the Industrial Revolution, many people had good paying jobs. They had money to buy what they needed. Good jobs included **textile mill**bosses, lawyers, and teachers. The number of schools grew. More people were able to go to school for the first time.

But the Industrial Revolution also caused suffering. **Factory** workers suffered. People who dug for**coal** suffered. They worked hard. But they did not make a lot of money. Whole families had to work to survive. Children often had to work, too.

Workers' pay

An adult factory worker might make between six and twelve dollars a week. Families had to spend at least ten dollars a week to live.

▼Working in a coal mine is a dangerous and dirty job.

Women at work

In the early 1800s, **textile mills** began hiring women. Women were hired to make cloth. The mills in Lowell, Massachusetts, were some of the first to hire women. Earning money made women feel better about themselves. "I shall be paid now for what I do," one twelve-year-old girl said happily.

The mill owners were happy, too. They paid women less than men. Women made less than half of what men got. Mill work was hard. Women worked at least twelve hours a day.

▼ *This is a photograph of Lowell, Massachusetts. Can you see the tall smokestacks?*

The women often lived in big company houses. The company houses had many rules. Their workers had to be in bed at a certain time. Visitors were closely watched. Women who broke those rules lost their jobs.

Women and young girls ▼ took jobs in textile mills.

Children at work

Poor children had worked in the past. They had worked on farms or in shops. During the Industrial Revolution, poor children began working in **factories**. Children also dug **coal**. Poor families needed their children to work. They needed their children's pay.

Children were paid less than adults for their work. A child would make about two dollars a week. Bosses started hiring children. They wanted to save money. Many bosses did not care about the children's safety.

▼ *These children speak out against working in factories.*

22

▲ Children often did the hardest, dirtiest jobs.

Joseph Hebergam was a seventeen-year-old **textile mill** worker. He used machines to make cloth. He had to stand all day working at a machine. His legs soon became weak. "In the morning[s], I could [barely] walk," he said in 1832.

Changing and Growing

The Industrial Revolution caused U.S. cities to grow quickly. Many people who moved to cities were **immigrants**. Immigrants are people who move from one country to another.

Farmers moved to the city as well. Immigrants and farmers worked in the new **factories**. They made goods in the factories.

Factory owners made workers work long hours. In some factories, workers could not take breaks. They had to keep working all the time. They were treated like machines.

These women are ▶
members of a union.

immigrant person who moves from one country to another
union group of people who try to improve working hours and pay

In 1866 some factory workers became fed up. They formed the first **unions**. Unions are groups of workers. They fight for fairer hours. They fight for better pay.

Today, most people work eight hours a day. That is much better than during the Industrial Revolution. Back then, people often had to work up to fourteen hours a day.

The Revolution goes on

Look around your house. The things you see there were all made using machines. Everything from cars to picture frames is made of **interchangeable parts**. This means they have parts that are the same size and shape. The Industrial Revolution gave us many great **products**.

The Industrial Revolution also did great harm. **Factories** dumped garbage into rivers. Burning **coal** dirtied the air.

Before the Industrial Revolution, people did not expect machines to help them. Today, we expect newer, better machines every year. Now we live with constant change. Each new machine seems to make change happen faster and faster. So, in a way, the Industrial Revolution is still with us.

Speaking in Dots and Dashes

Samuel F. B. Morse **invented** the **telegraph** in the 1830s. The telegraph is a machine that sends messages down an electric wire. The message is received by a telegraph operator. The operator uses a special code to read the message. This code is called **Morse Code**.

In Morse Code, each letter and number is represented by dots, dashes, and spaces. For instance, the message to signal trouble is SOS. The code is three dots for S (...), three dashes for O (---), and another three dots for S (...).

▼ *This is a telegraph machine. It punched the Morse Code dots and dashes into thin strips of paper.*

Morse Code	code made of dots, dashes, and spaces that is used to send telegraph messages
telegraph	machine that sends messages down an electric wire

This is a picture of ▶
Samuel Morse.

In the past, Morse Code was used to send messages quickly. Now we have telephones and e-mail.

Below you will see the Morse Code alphabet and numbers. Can you write your name in Morse Code?

▼ *This chart shows Morse Code.*

A .-	B -...	C -.-.	D -..	E .	F ..-.	G --.	H	I ..	J .---
K -.-	L .-..	M --	N -.	O ---	P .--.	Q --.-	R .-.	S ...	T -
U ..-	V ...-	W .--	X -..-	Y -.--	Z --..				
0 -----	1 .----	2 ..---	3 ...--	4 ....-	5	6 -....	7 --...	8 ---..	9 ----.

▼ *Who invented the telegraph?*

...	.-	--	..-	.	.-..
S	A	M	U	E	L

--	---	.-.	...	.
M	O	R	S	E

Glossary

American System way of using interchangeable parts to produce goods

carpenter someone who makes things with wood

coal black or brown rock that burns well

factory building where products are made

fuel something that is burned to make power or heat

immigrant person who moves from one country to another

industrial anything that has to do with making products (things that are made and sold)

interchangeable parts parts that are the exact same size and shape

invent create something that has never been made before

iron tough metal that is easily shaped when hot

Morse Code code made of dots, dashes, and spaces that is used to send telegraph messages

oil dark liquid that burns well

plow tool used to cut the ground for planting crops

product thing that is made and sold

railroad business that uses trains to move people and things

revolution time of great change

spinning jenny machine that spins many threads at once

spinning wheel wheel used to make thread

steam engine machine that heats up water to make steam

steel strong metal created by combining iron with other metals

telegraph machine that sends messages down an electric wire

textile mill building with machines that make cloth

union group of people who try to improve working hours and pay

Want to Know More?

Books to read

- Connolly, Sean. *The Industrial Revolution*. Chicago: Heinemann Library, 2003.
- Woog, Adam. *A Sweatshop During the Industrial Revolution*. San Diego: Lucent, 2002.

Websites

- http://americanhistory.si.edu/ exhibitions/exhibition.cfm?key=38& exkey=51

  "Engines of Change: The American Industrial Revolution, 1790–1860" is an exhibition at the Smithsonian's National Museum of American History. Learn all about it at this site.

- http://www.uml.edu/tsongas/ index2.htm

  Tsongas Industrial History Center offers tours that show what life was like in the Lowell textile mills. Learn all about it at this site.

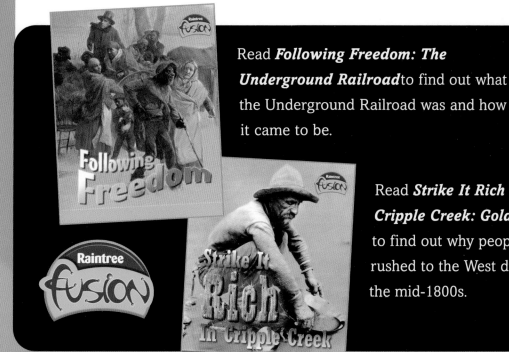

Read **Following Freedom: The Underground Railroad** to find out what the Underground Railroad was and how it came to be.

Read **Strike It Rich in Cripple Creek: Gold Rush** to find out why people rushed to the West during the mid-1800s.

Index